C000006163

Simple
Steps to
Happiness

by the best-selling author of *A Winning Attitude*

SIMPLE STEPS TO HAPPINESS

Copyright © Rosie Hamilton-McGinty 2008

All rights reserved.

The right of Rosie Hamilton-McGinty to be identified as the author of this work has been asserted in accordance with sections 77 and 78 of the Copyright, Designs and Patents Act 1988.

Summersdale Publishers Ltd
46 West Street
Chichester
West Sussex
PO19 1RP
UK

www.summersdale.com

Printed and bound in Great Britain

ISBN: 978-1-84024-660-5

To my twin grandsons
Angus and Hamish.
Your happiness and laughter
light up the room and
I feel privileged to be
your grandma.

Contents

Introduction

Someone once said to me that people are as happy as they make up their minds to be. I believe that happiness is paramount in our daily lives, and that everyone feels more comfortable being around a happy person.

I have given you some simple guidelines for ways to enrich your life and replace feelings of unhappiness in a very short space of time with feelings of love and happiness.

You can use this book in different ways; read it from start to finish, or perhaps read a simple step each day and try to live it out, or just have it to hand to dip into every so often.

Believe
in
yourself

The first step to personal happiness is to truly believe in yourself, your talents, your abilities, your gifts and your personal power.

Seek happiness in all aspects
of your life – take joy in your
relationships with family and
friends, delight in your working
environment and look for the best in
yourself and your body.

Happiness is achieved
when you live by and demonstrate
the three Rs: respect for yourself,
respect for others and responsibility
for all your actions.

Trust your intuition – the little voices inside that guide you.

Love the body you're in because it's the only one you've got. If you're happy on the inside it will show on the outside.

Make your social environment work for you and not against you – if you surround yourself with negative influences and people, their outworn thoughts and behaviour will hold you back in life.

Stop worrying!

Never dwell on your fears –
remember that they are only thoughts
which can be changed within
seconds by thinking more positively
and taking manageable steps to
diminish them.

Stop worrying – it won't achieve anything other than making you ill. Every problem has a solution.

Motivate yourself into action – success begins by taking the first step.

When feeling sad and
downhearted, have the power and
belief to pick yourself up and start
over again.

Show enthusiasm for everything
you do in order to gain the maximum
benefits from every situation you
encounter and every challenge
you face.

Strive to do better – continue
to set higher standards for yourself.
Watch your confidence and happiness
flourish as you achieve your goals.

Avoid petty arguments and
squabbles. Instead of quarrelling,
try to use constructive criticism to
resolve disagreements.

Sharing happiness

Be generous in your dealings with others – offer your time, a compliment or a favour and make a mental note of how good this feels.

Make every person you speak to
feel special; being attentive and
kind will lead to new and
rewarding friendships.

Reminisce with old friends and recall happy childhood memories; it's a great way to lift your spirits and keep focussed on all the good things life has to offer.

Treat people with respect – more
rewards and happiness will come
back to you when you show others
you respect them.

Happiness is achieved when
you open your heart to kindness and
love – show the people in your life
how grateful you are to have them.

Volunteer your time regardless of how busy you are. Try to put your friends before the trivialities of life.

Treat others the way you wish to be treated yourself.

Happiness is achieved when your actions help and assist others to realise and reach their full potential.

Talking to elderly relatives or acquaintances about their lives will not only make them feel special, but also give you a greater appreciation of your ability to overcome the challenges life may throw at you.

Happiness comes from
giving your friends and loved ones
enough love to stay connected,
but enough space to gently grow
as individuals.

Let go –
change
your habits

A lot of our unhappiness comes from living in the past, thus preventing us from fully living and appreciating the present and making plans for the future.

We manufacture our own unhappiness by focussing on unhappy thoughts. Replace with pleasant thoughts of love, kindness and goodwill.

Take time to just be, relax
and stay silent for a few minutes.
Happiness is about being at peace
with yourself.

Don't dwell on bad experiences
or problems from the past. Instead
focus on the good things in your
life and on making your future
much brighter.

Happiness comes from
sharing your knowledge with others
– use what you have learnt through
your experiences to help friends
during difficult times.

Try something new – if you don't love your work then you shouldn't be doing it. Change direction to something you feel passionate about.

Accept others for who they are
and not who you want them to be.

Take action

We all make mistakes. The important
thing is to recognise when you have
made a mistake and to take action to
put it right.

Happiness comes when you open your arms to change and new experiences – without letting go of your values.

Don't let bad habits hold you back. Realising your behaviour is having a negative impact on your life means you're one step closer to changing it for the better.

Happiness comes from putting your hand up and admitting you were wrong: don't let a little dispute and your own stubbornness ruin a great relationship.

Remove negative influences from your life; recognise the source of your stress – it could be a person, work environment or a relationship.

Try to live an exciting life full of new experiences and adventure rather than never trying anything new for fear of the unknown.

It's only natural for life to have its ups and downs. Appreciate the good times so that you can guide yourself through the tough times knowing things will get better.

Transform your habitual thinking – happiness comes from letting go of outworn patterns and negative thoughts which keep us stuck in the past.

De-clutter your mind of
negative and unhappy feelings and
make space for new positive thoughts
and exciting plans for the future.

Respond to situations with a positive state of mind – see every problem as an opportunity for change for the better.

Find inner peace – if you
achieve this you will have found
ultimate happiness.

Take advice from successful
people – this will help you feel
empowered and motivated
to achieve.

Change your attitude and approach to meeting new people – be encouraged to join new groups, expand your horizons and stretch yourself.

Make a stronger commitment
to yourself – put yourself first and
watch the opportunities come your
way. Be committed to achieving your
goals and approach any obstacles as
opportunities to show how capable
you are to yourself and others.

*Count your
blessings*

Happiness comes from
realising just how fortunate you are.

Many *of life's little problems are put in perspective when seeing smiling faces of young children and babies.*

Happiness comes from sharing
what you have with others who are
less fortunate.

Really get to know yourself
– self-awareness helps you to develop
self-belief and inner power.

Identify and manage
your stress – learn to take time
out to relax and create a more
balanced life.

Happiness is achieved
when you start saying 'I believe
everything is now improving' and
meaning what you say.

Trust your intuition, do what feels
right for you – you know yourself best.

Move forward

Never doubt your abilities.
You are a capable person. Every
individual has their own unique
qualities and talents, and this
includes you.

Surround yourself with
positive thinking people – they boost
your energy levels and stop you
feeling insecure about yourself.

If you focus on happy thoughts in times of worry or stress, your attitude towards the problem will be more productive.

Set yourself a challenge – research shows that when you have something in life to aim for it makes you feel happier.

Have a belief – whether in
some spiritual entity or in yourself.

Be proud of who you are – your
relationships, your behaviour and
your achievements.

Give life your all – the more you offer to the world the more you will receive in return.

Make the decision to move forward in life – pick yourself up from a bad experience and jump into the next chapter.

Overcome your fear of
change and embrace the variety of
opportunities that life has to offer.

Take responsibility for your
future, steer your life to where you
want it to go.

Everyday happiness

Begin each day being happy – you
have a choice to be happy or unhappy.
Remember a person is just about as
happy as they choose to be.

Act positively to every person you
are in contact with – your attitude is
what marks your character.

Always be willing to give time
to others – remember what you give
out comes back multiplied.

Enjoy *being with your family*
– a loving atmosphere in your home
is the foundation of a happy life.

Working and getting
along with others can produce
great results.

A person who exercises regularly,
eats properly and behaves responsibly
can't help but feel happy.

Spend time with loved ones;
make time for conversation over a
meal, walk or share special moments
together. These simple pleasures will
bring priceless happiness.

Try to avoid gossip – talk about people but always speak positively, particularly in their absence.

Never compromise – *you deserve the best.*

Everyone is a little shy so
take the initiative to make the first
move or greet someone – reaching out
to someone will make you feel good.

Happiness comes when others can love you just the way you are and don't try to change you.

Happiness is a state of mind

Find a purpose in life; know
what you're here for and fulfil that
role to the best of your ability.

Take charge of your daily
choices, your actions and your future.

Happiness comes from
reaping the rewards and benefits of
your hard work.

Be happy to enjoy each day in the present rather than always fixating on the future.

Happiness comes from within – from your thoughts and your emotions. Start now to change your thoughts, always think positively and strive for success.

True happiness comes from shared experiences with friends and loved ones.

Happiness and success go hand in hand, and can be achieved by changing one's attitude towards others.

Happiness is linked with self-esteem – work on spiritual self-awareness to improve your self-image and ultimately your confidence.

Smile! *A smile breaks down barriers and a big sincere smile melts away any opposition.*

Happiness comes from
*speaking up for yourself – have your
say and feel your confidence grow.*

The perfect recipe for a happier self

You can achieve everything you desire. Just visualise it, believe in yourself and go for it.

***Make** plans for all the things you wish to accomplish over the next week, month and year.*

Be happy that you don't have all the answers – life is mysterious and exciting so embrace the fact that you don't know what's around the corner. No one else does!

Think big – *the sky is the limit.*

Balance your life with work and leisure – the perfect recipe for a happier self.

Some people say that happiness is about leaving a legacy and doing something that is important for humanity. Think about what differences you can make.

Happiness is the ultimate goal for every individual. If you asked most people they would all want similar things: emotional and financial security, a loving relationship, and to make a difference.

Happiness is a state of mind
– we all have a right to happiness
and to enjoy a long and fulfilling life.

Happiness and love are the
keys to all your successes in life – the
way you are and what you give out
comes back to you eventually, only
multiplied in size.

Live simply – *enjoy walking,
talking and being with friends.
This is what personal fulfilment is
all about.*

Take time to remember all
the wonderful things you have
experienced in your life. What an
incredible journey you have been on
so far!

Finally – relax, read this book again and you will soon be thinking more confidently and positively about yourself. You will realise that the basis for true happiness is about being loving and caring to others. Try it for a week and see...

Positive affirmations

Begin each new day with positive affirmations to build a mental picture of how you want your life to be. You can think up your own or use these for an everyday boost.

'*I am happier now that I
believe in myself*'

'*I trust that life is sending me all the
opportunities I need to change
my life*'

*'I am attracting
successful relationships'*

*'My attitude to others is
improving daily'*

'I am now giving the best of myself to others unconditionally'

'My life is improving by the minute'

'I am now at peace with myself'

*'I feel happy and confident
about myself'*

'*I believe in MYSELF*'

'*I am grateful for all I have achieved
in my life*'

The way to happiness

Keep your heart free from hate
Your mind from worry
Live simply, expect little, give much
Fill your life with love
Scatter sunshine, forget self,
think of others
Do as you would be done by

A little about Rosie ...and her vision

My purpose is to help individuals develop self-belief, self-awareness, and to discover their purpose in life. From this position of security one can move forward, make necessary changes, step out of habitual comfort zones and subsequently develop new positive approaches and attitudes that encourage success, happiness and personal fulfilment.

I am currently studying for a Masters Degree at the University of Brighton with a dissertation entitled 'Spirituality into Organisations' via the **A Winning Attitude Program.**

A Winning Attitude Program *is beneficial to individuals, groups and organisations in understanding how a person can develop themselves, their character ethics, self-belief and self-awareness. This raised self-awareness among staff leads to improved team and management performance.*

For information on one-to-one consultations, presentations and training please contact:

e-mail: info@awinningattitude.com

www.awinningattitude.com

Rosie Hamilton-McGinty

A Winning Attitude

TO CHANGE YOUR LIFE – CHANGE YOUR ATTITUDE

A WINNING ATTITUDE
To Change Your Life – Change Your Attitude

Rosie Hamilton-McGinty

£2.99   Paperback   ISBN: 978 1 84024 404 5

With *A Winning Attitude*, you can:

- motivate and guide yourself
- be in control of yourself, your appetite, your passion
- do right by others
- keep emotions under control
- open the way to empathy, to real listening, to taking another person's perspective. Empathy leads to caring and compassion.

Take control of yourself and your life; take up a winning attitude.

'This little book could give you a whole new outlook on life'

BRIGHTON EVENING ARGUS

the
formula

the secret to
a better life

geoff thompson